I0469848

Select Images

JH Fleming

Joseph Fleming

Original Photography

Decades of being around accomplished talent producing absolutely phenomenal quality work has taught that we are capable of greatness. It is possible to meet our destiny and become it. Experiencing excellence done with such apparent ease and humble selfless gratification is the motivation for this photography. Most important was having the freedom.

Being colorblind gives an advantage when composing black & white... less confusion.
This special collection selected from thousands of captures. All images were framed
in the camera and presented without edits, genuine as seen through the lens.
Panchromatic conversion applied by unique proprietary process.

Limited prints and custom work available.

info@ BEACHNOISE.com

JH FLEMING

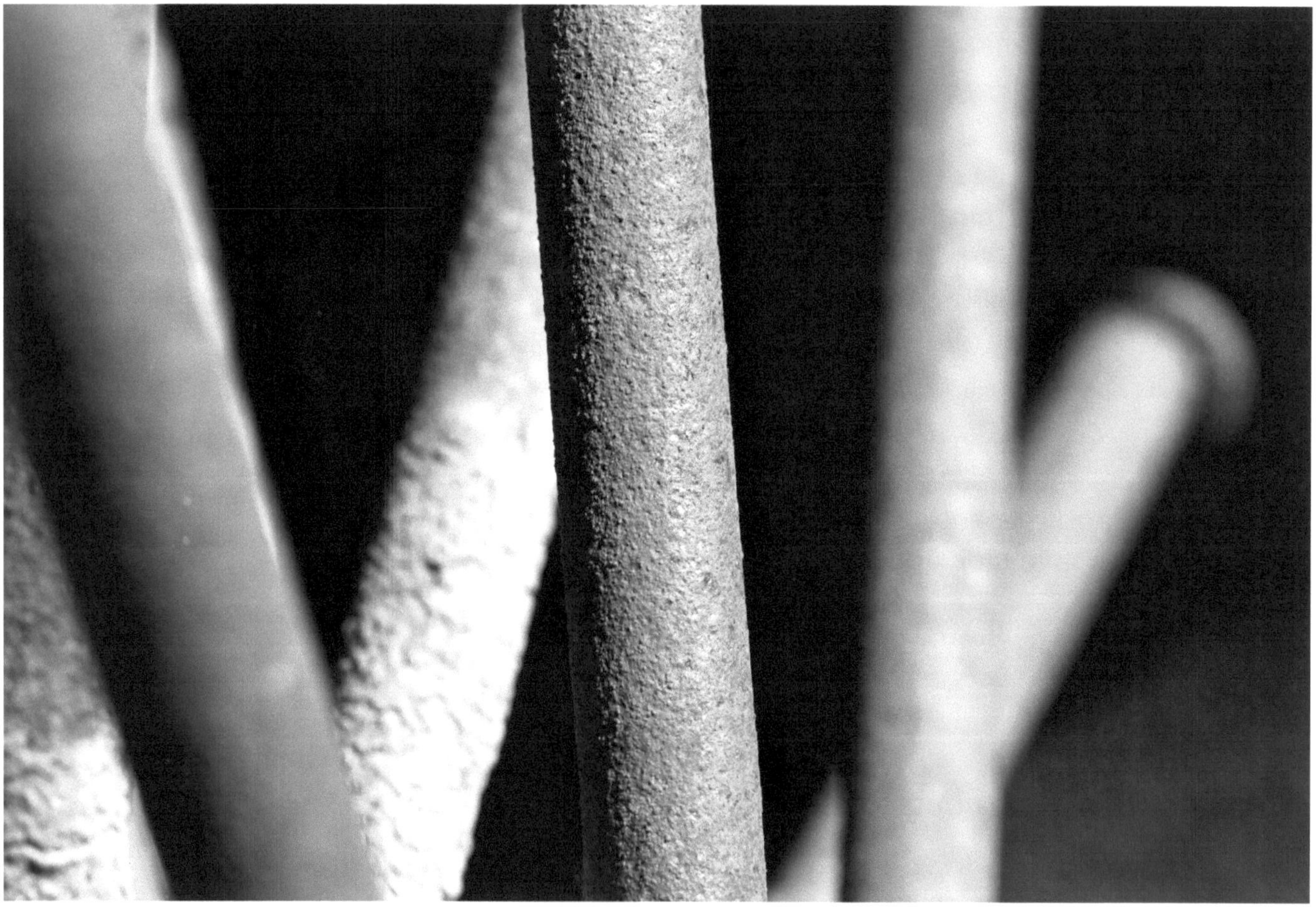

0780

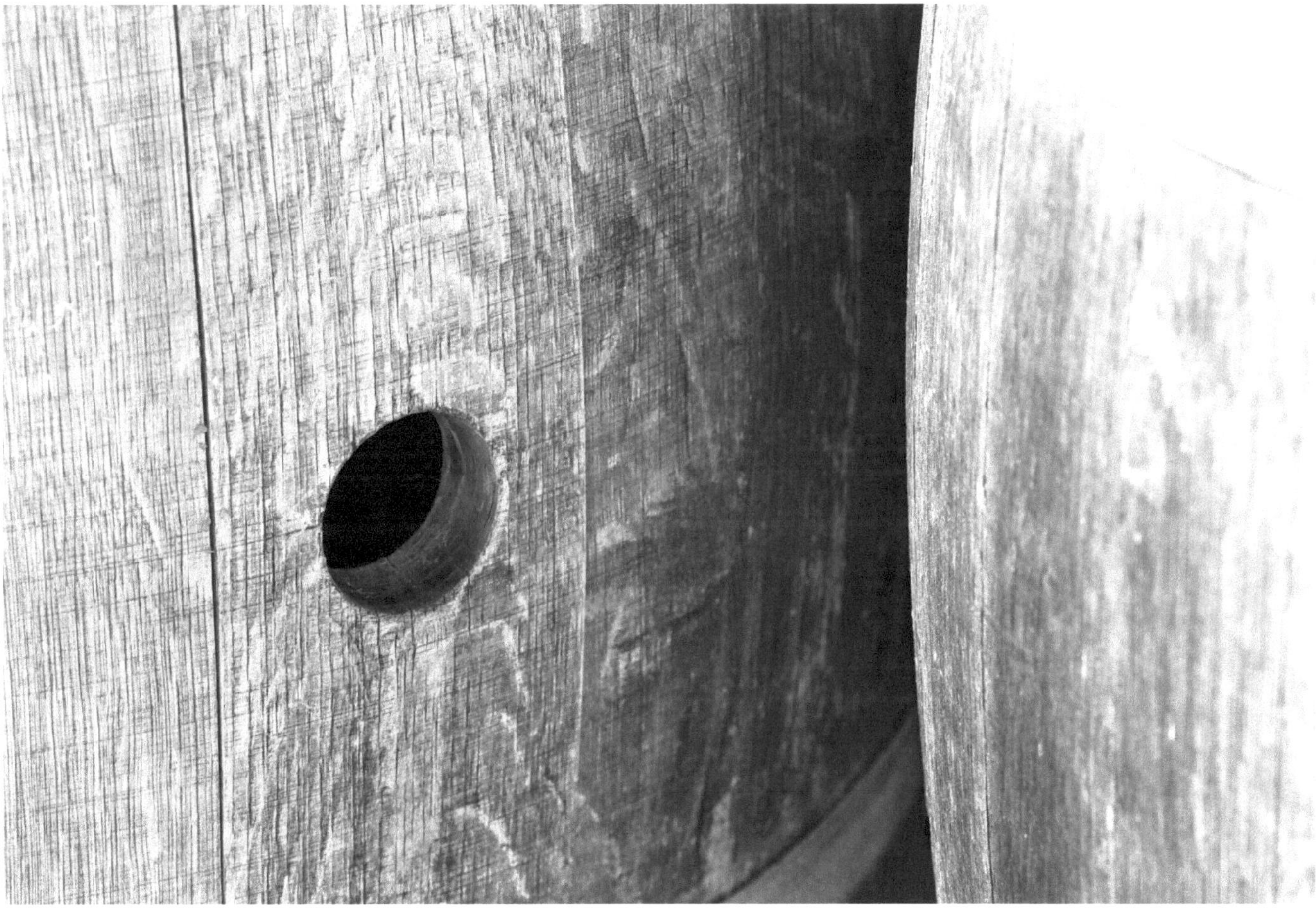

0826

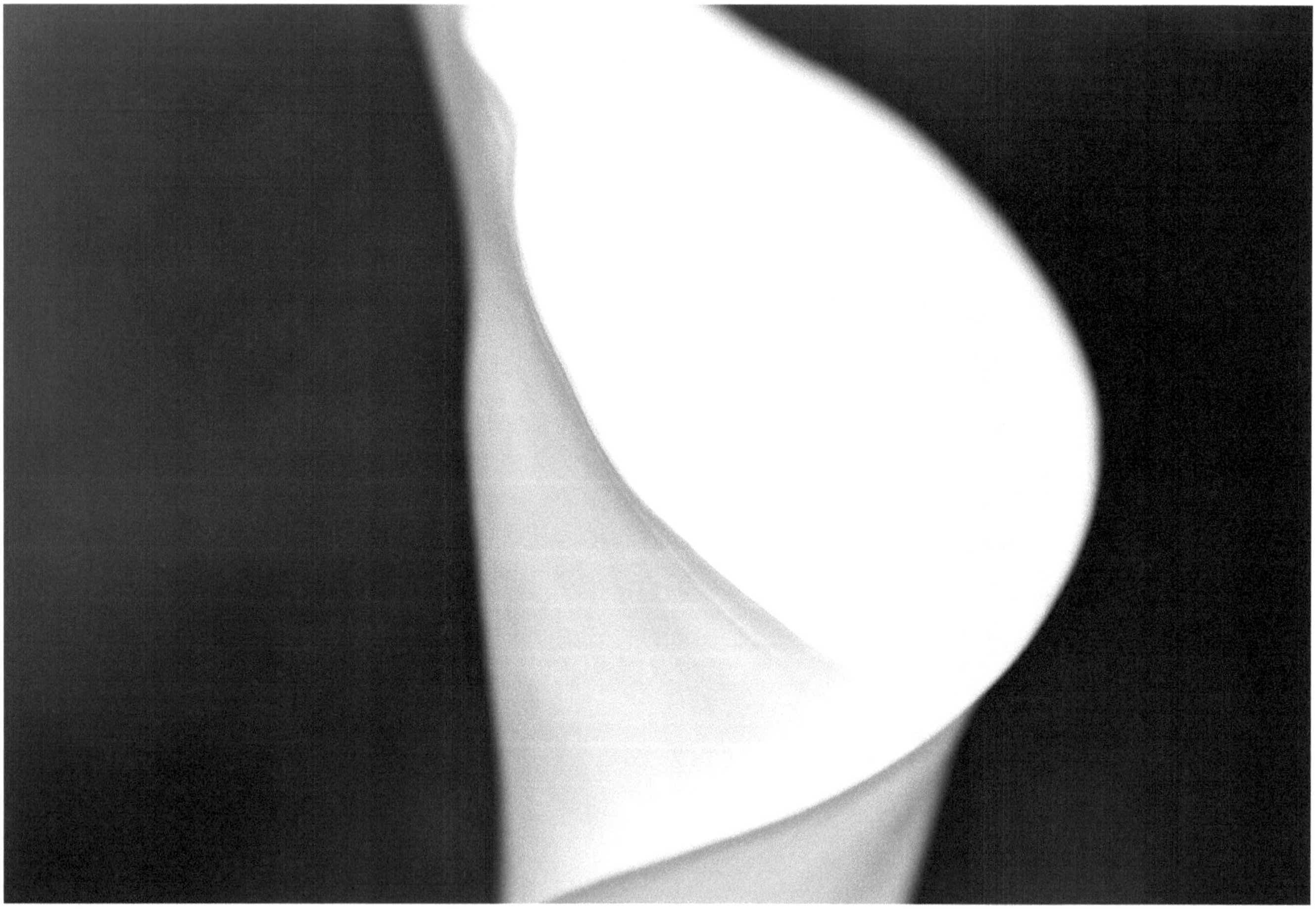

0920

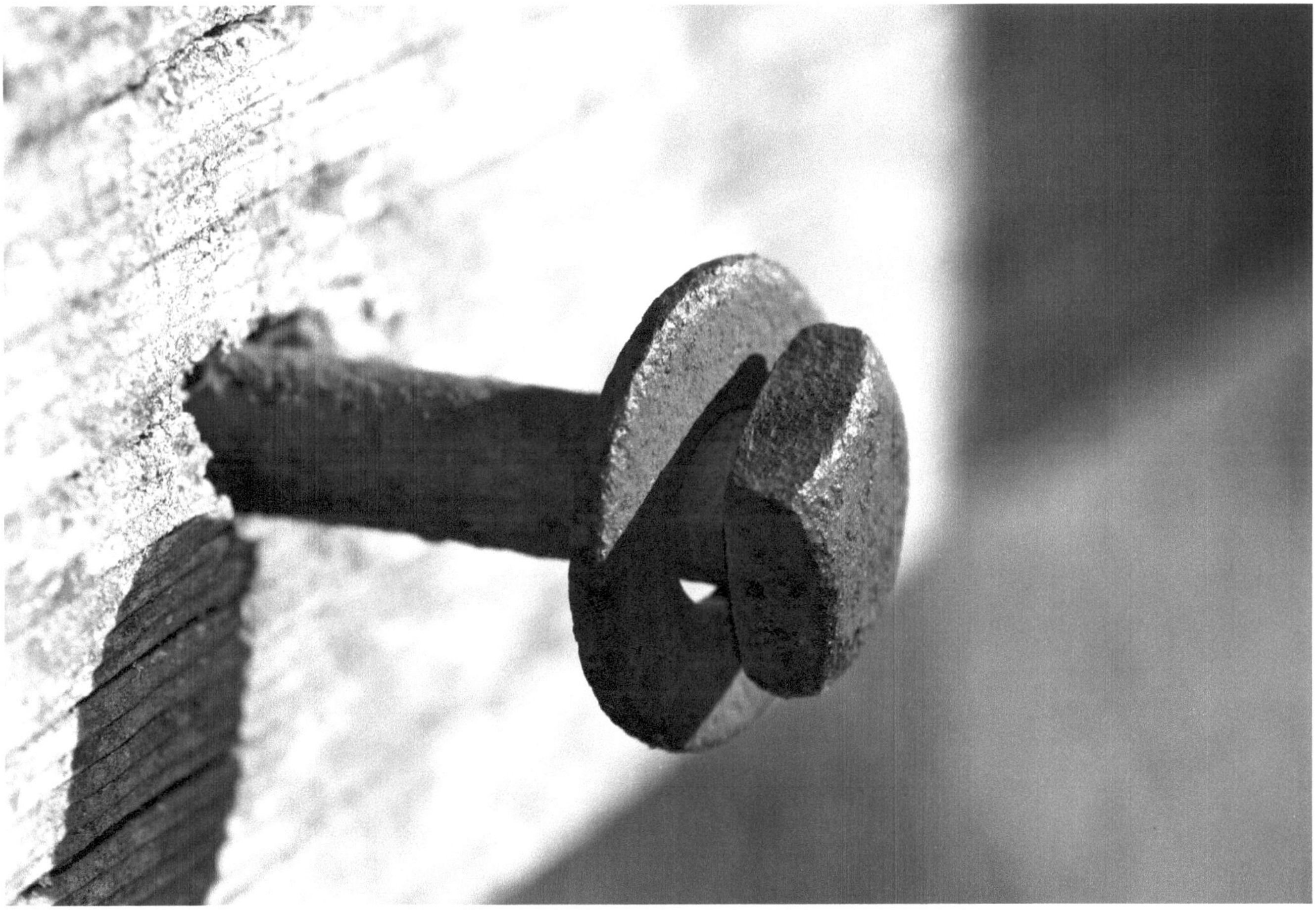

1173

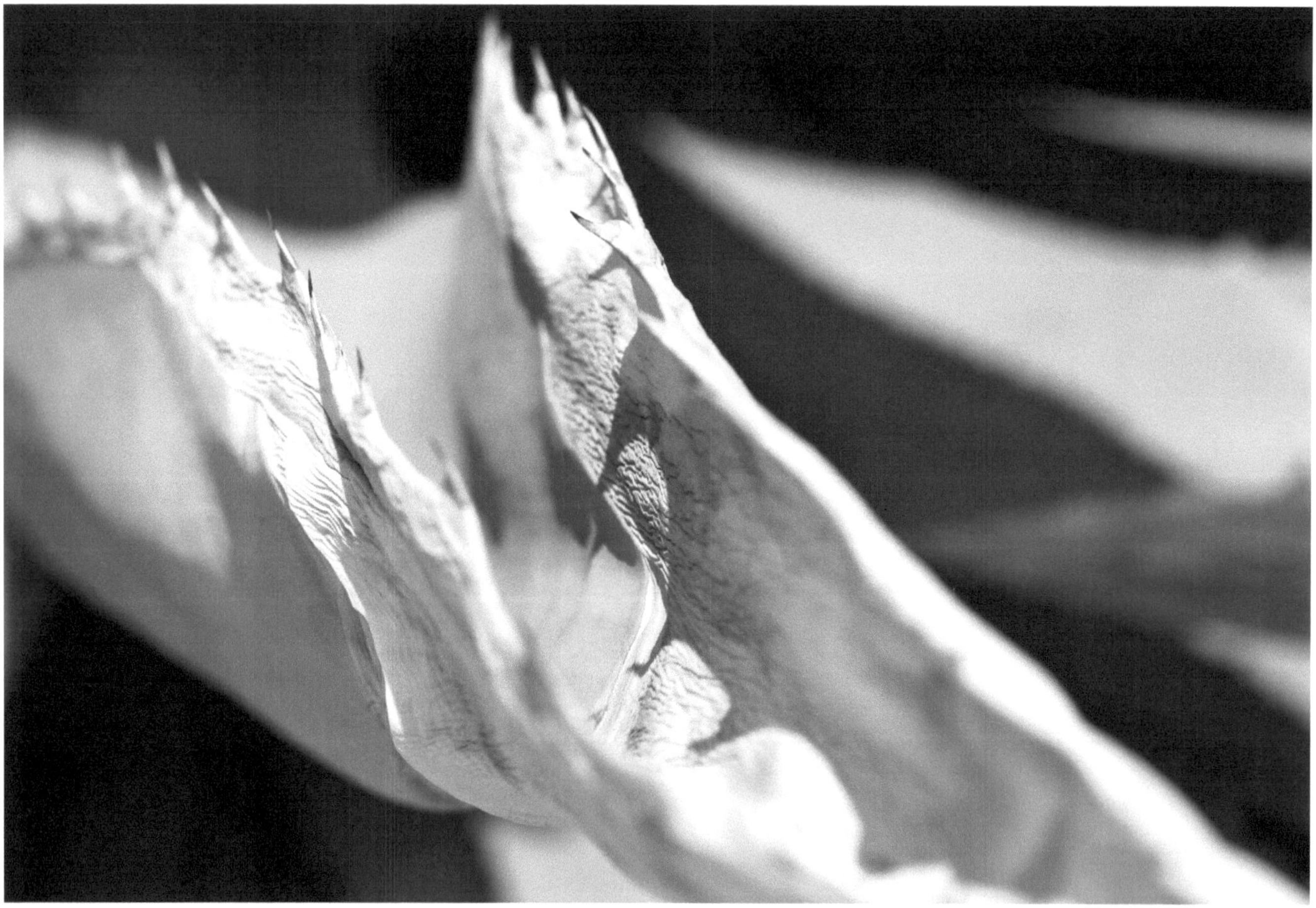

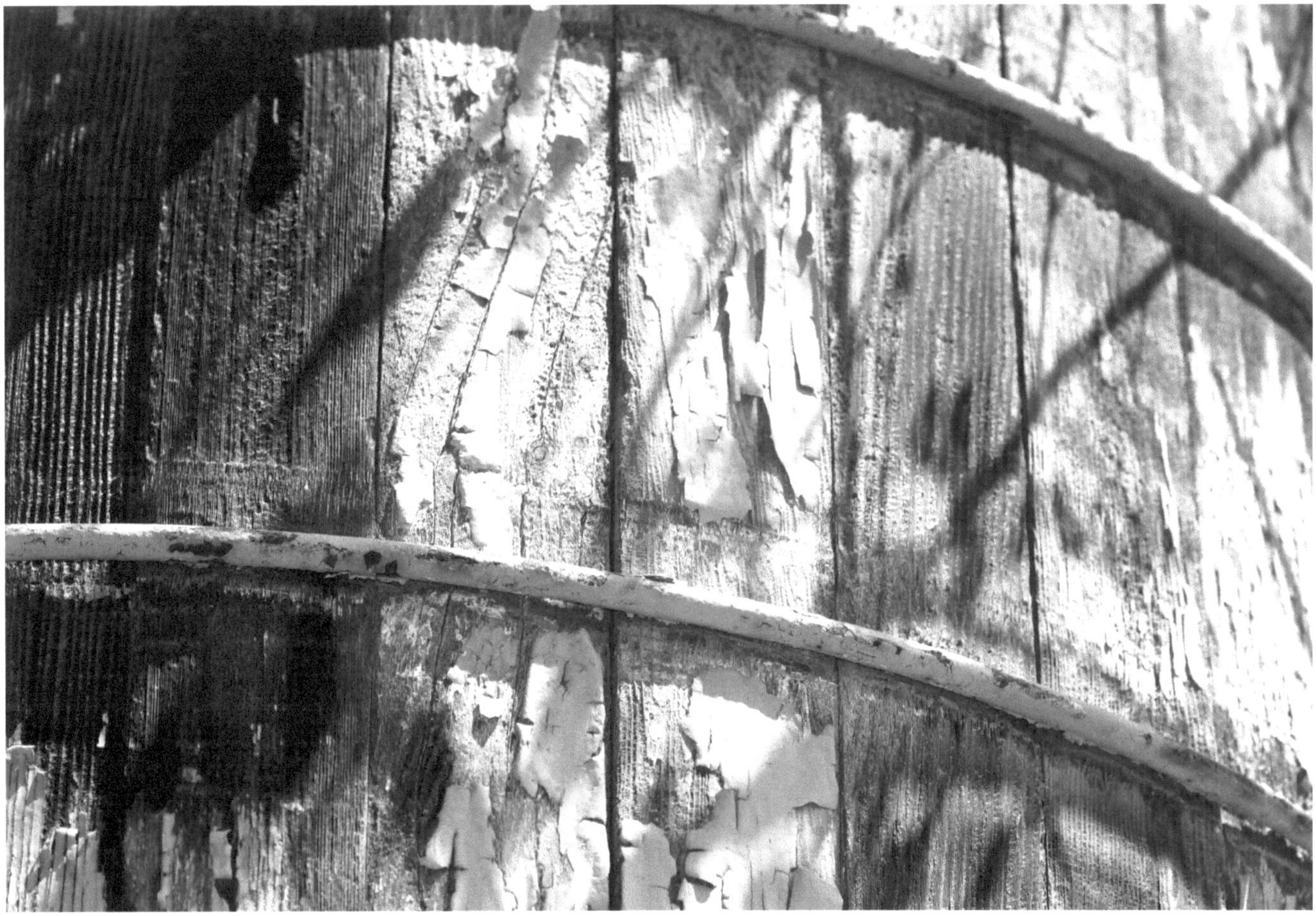
1608

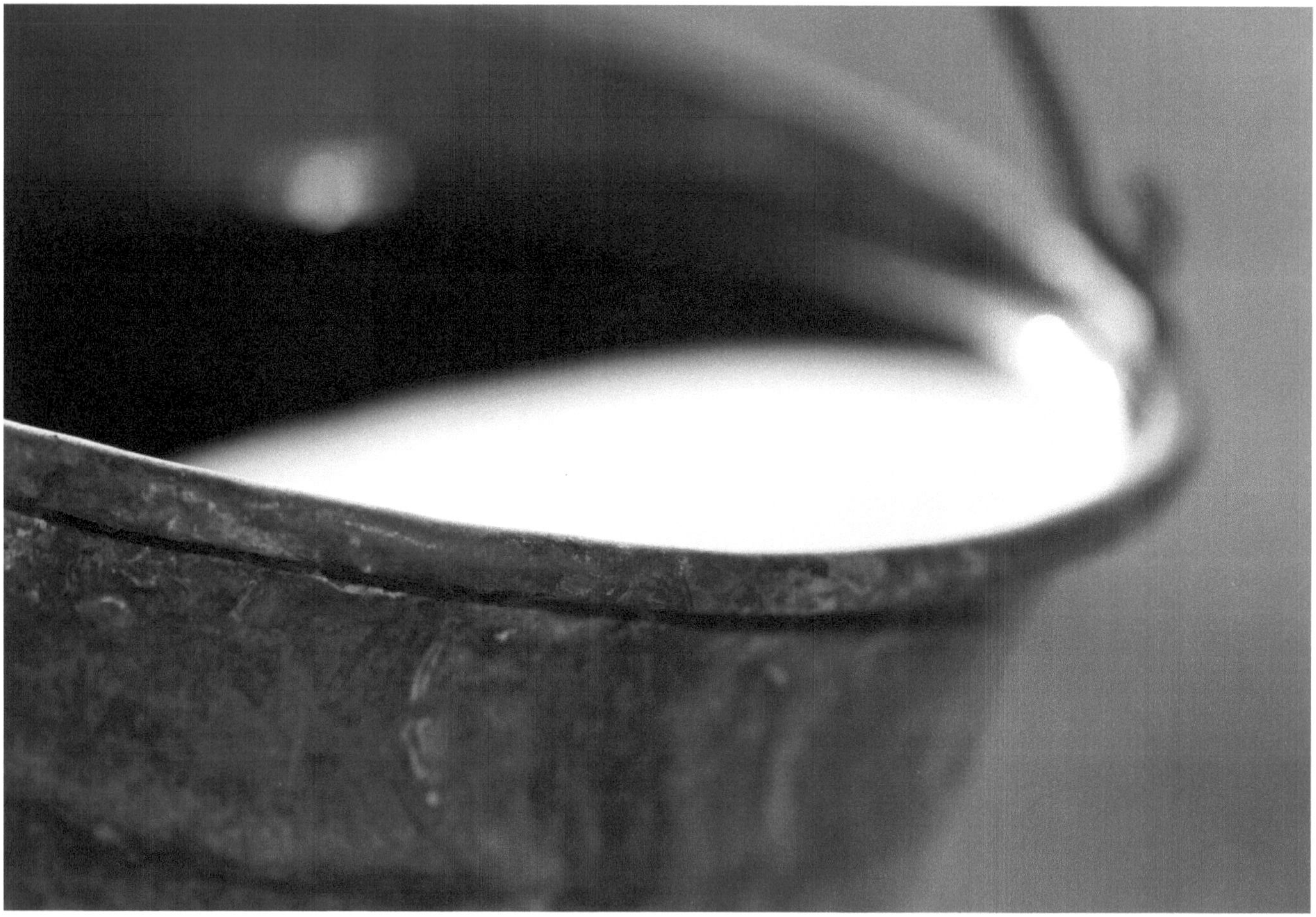

2180

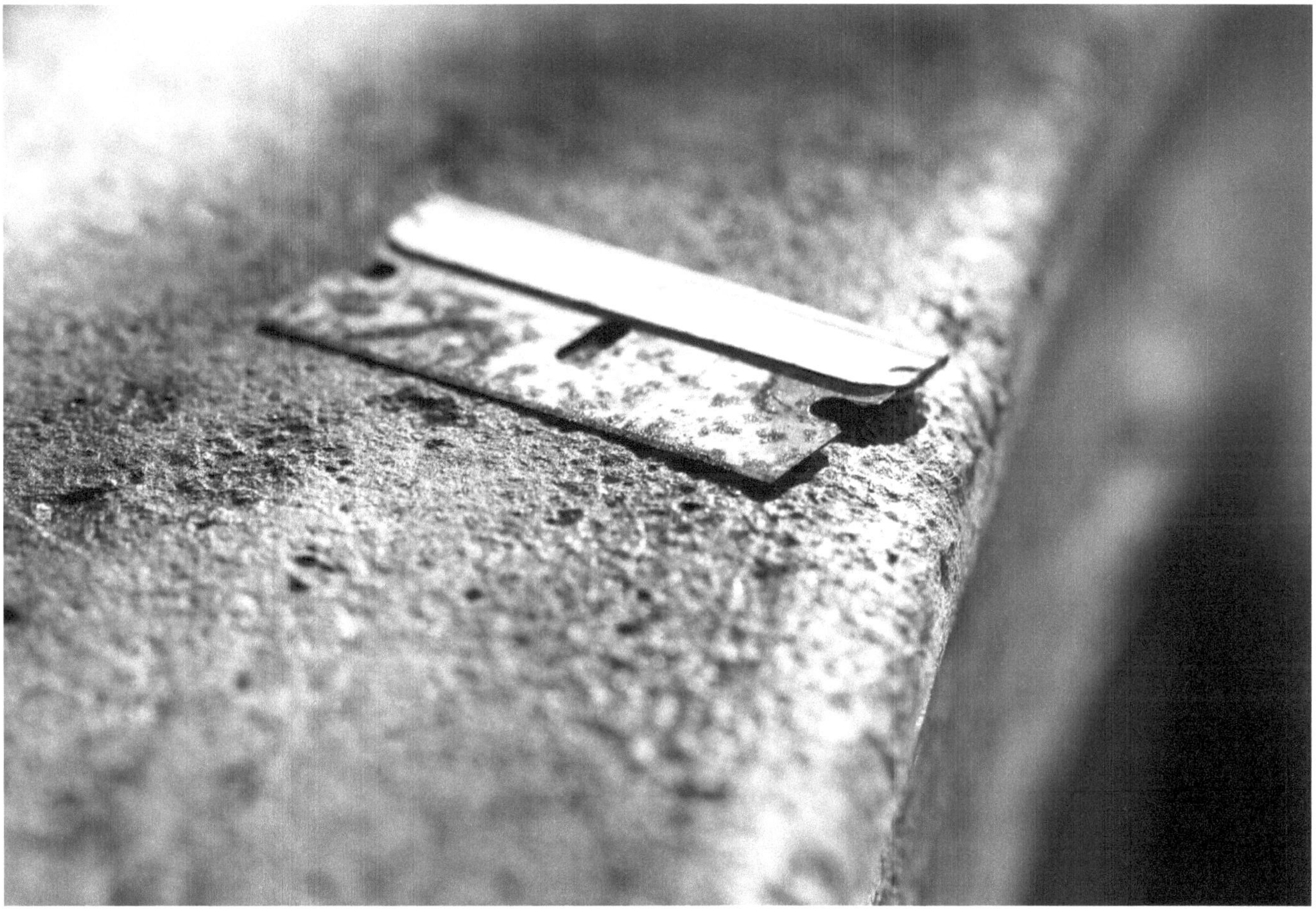

2467

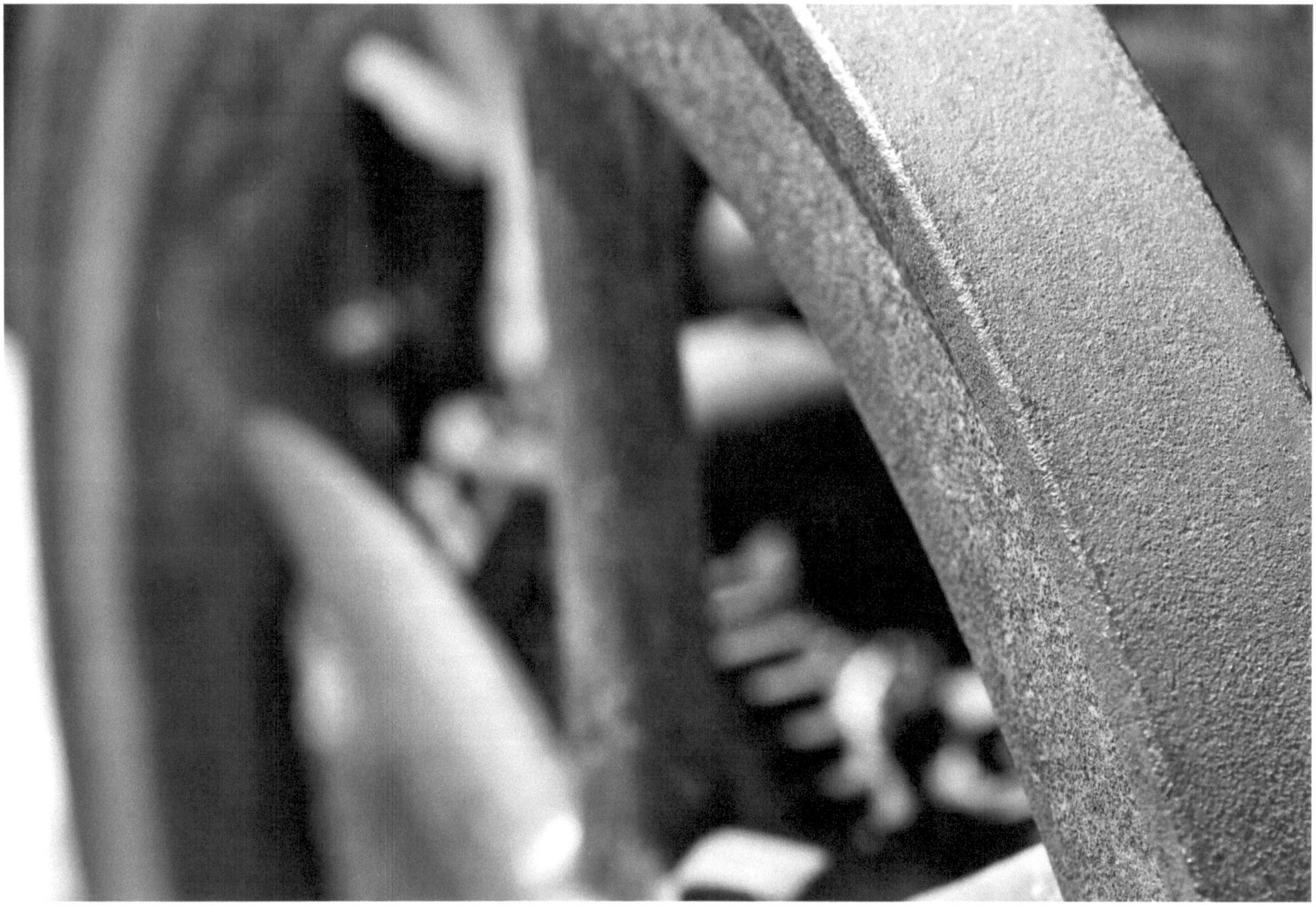

2962

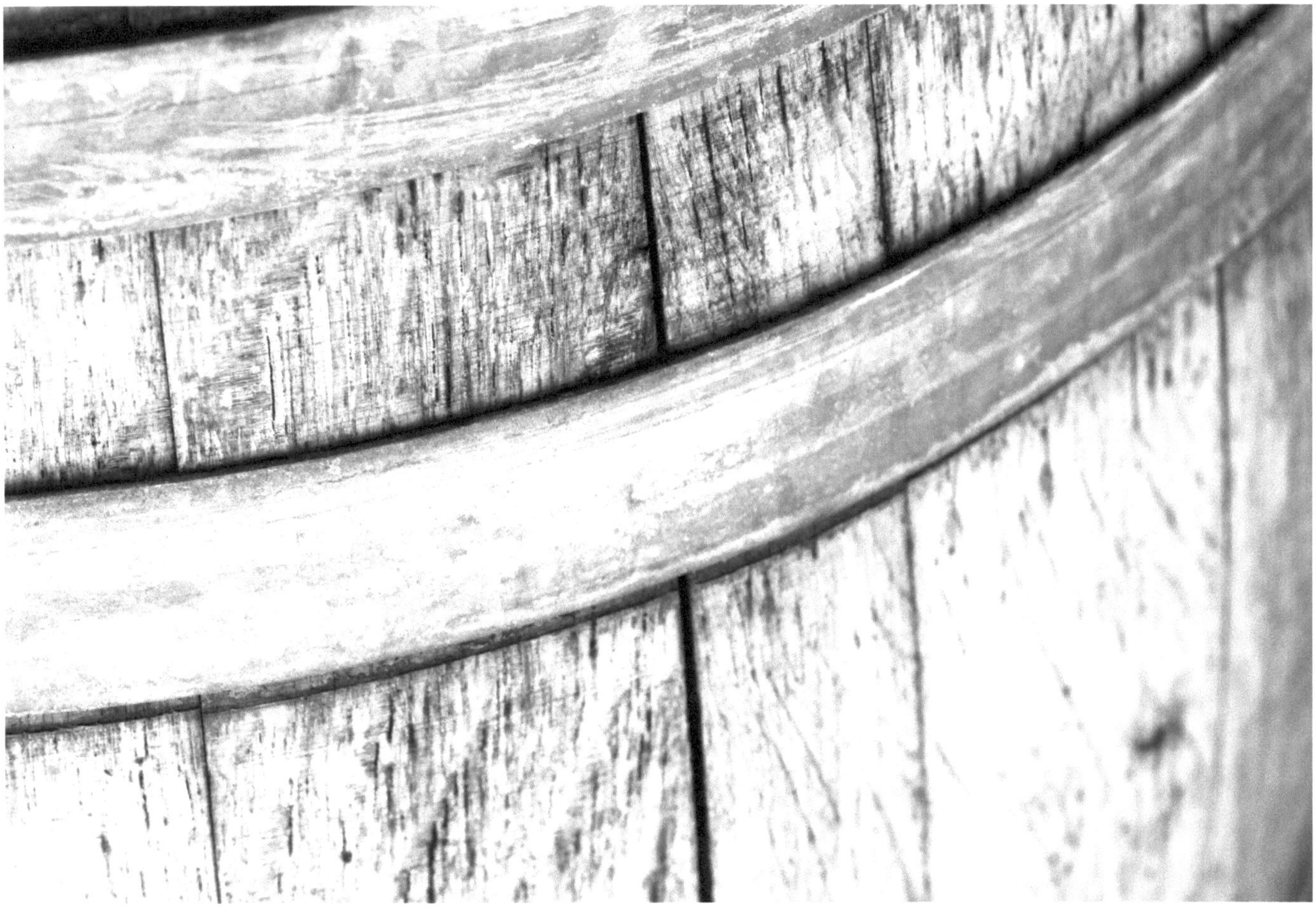

3151

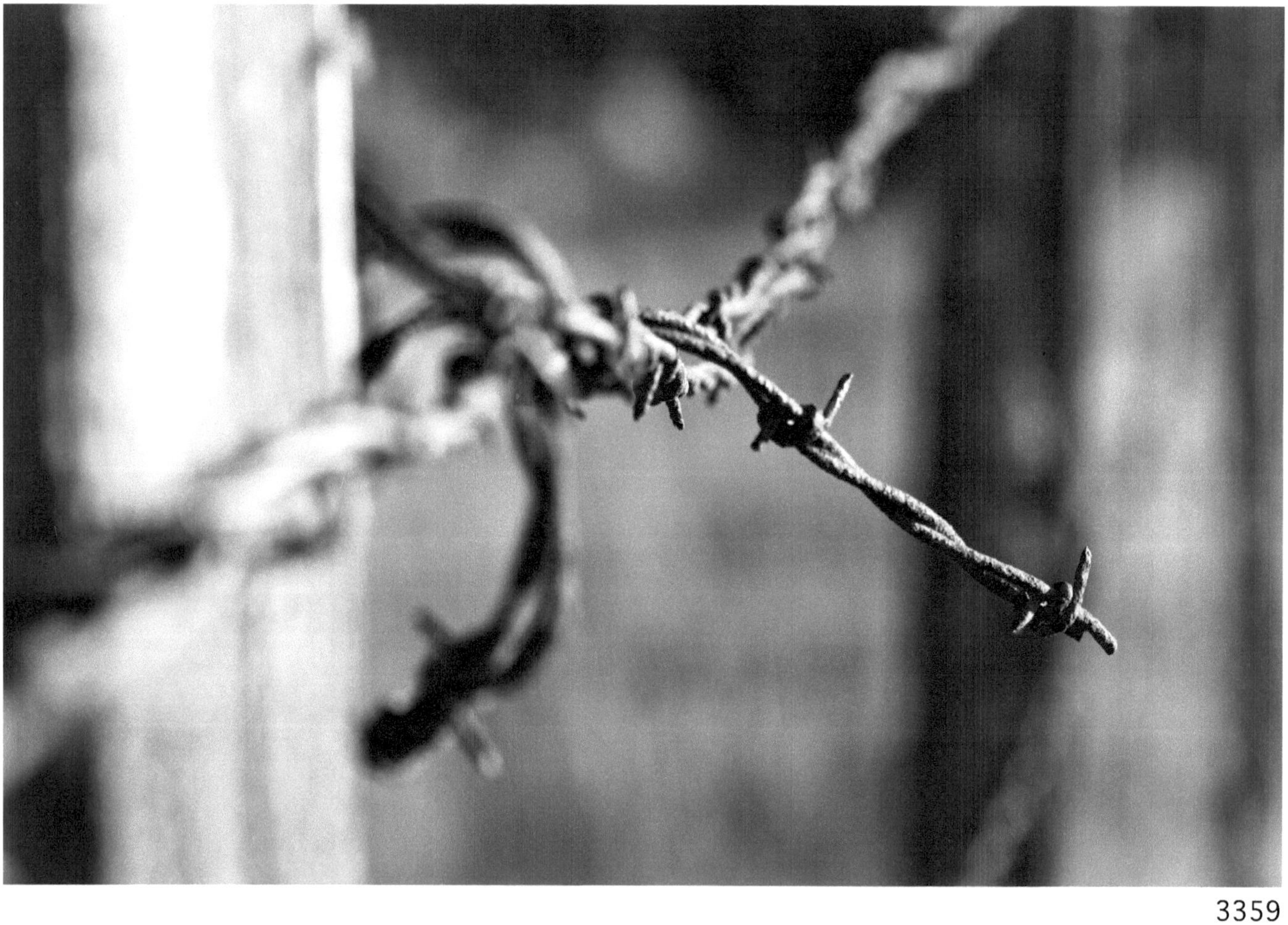

3359

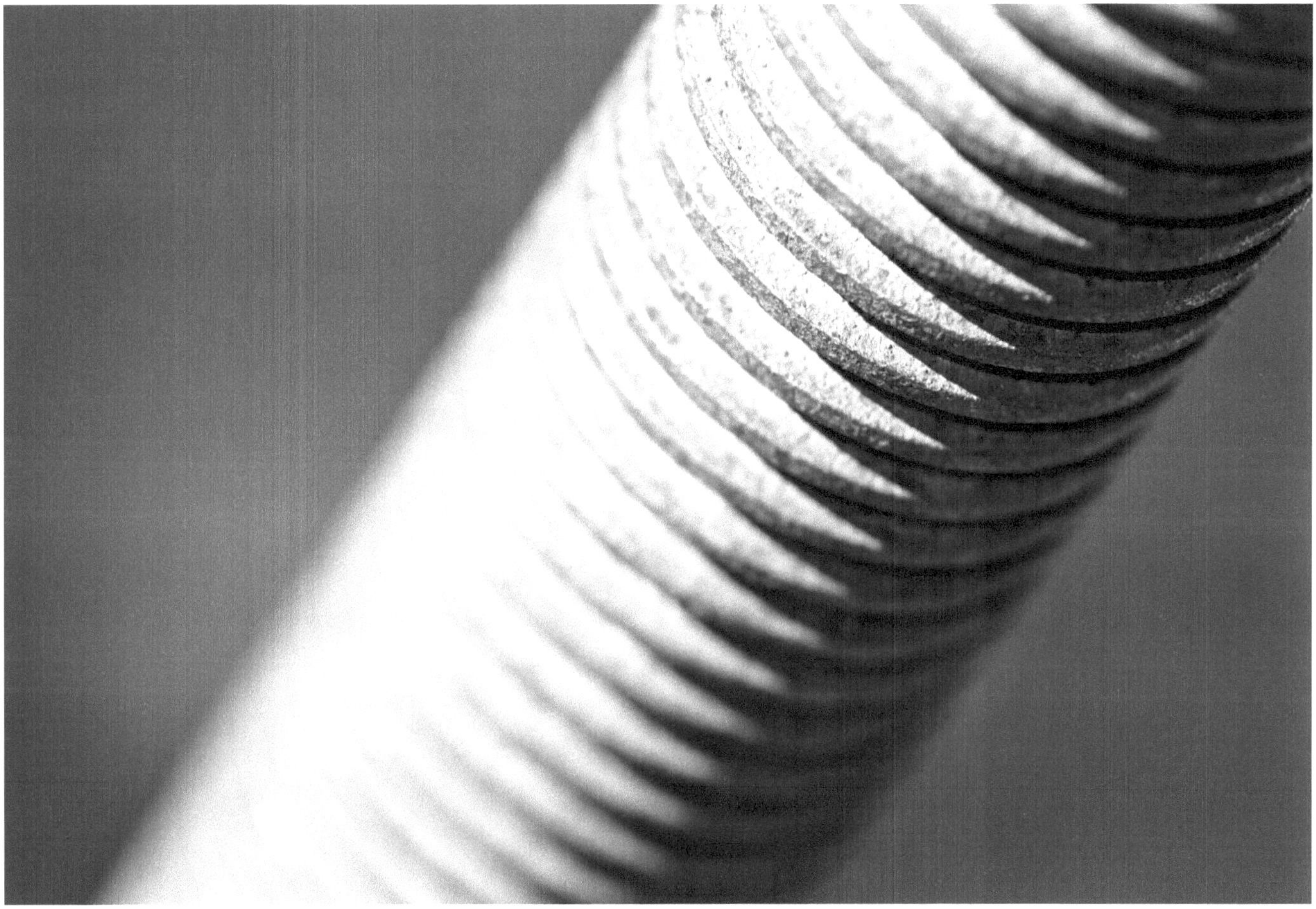
3937

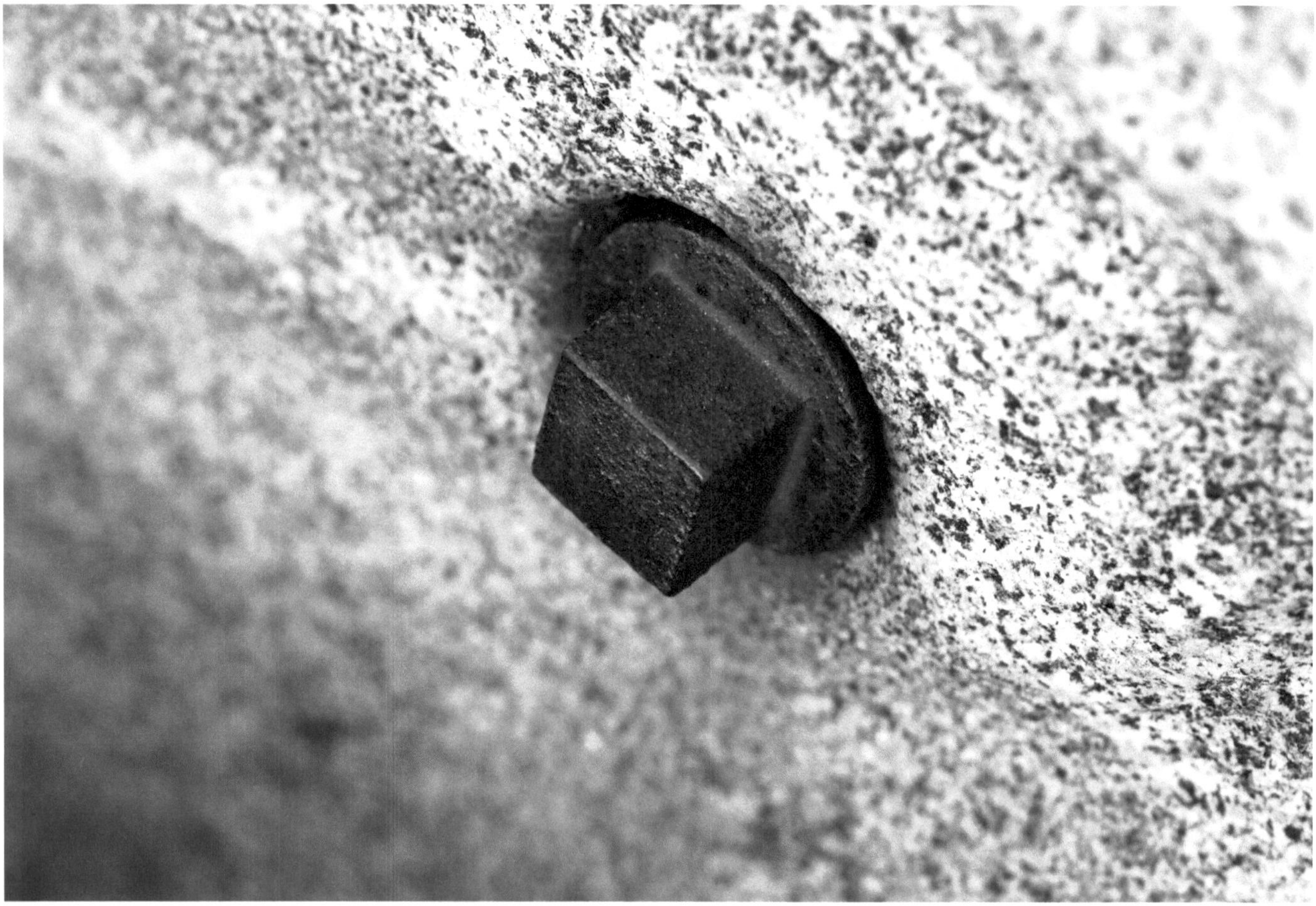

4035

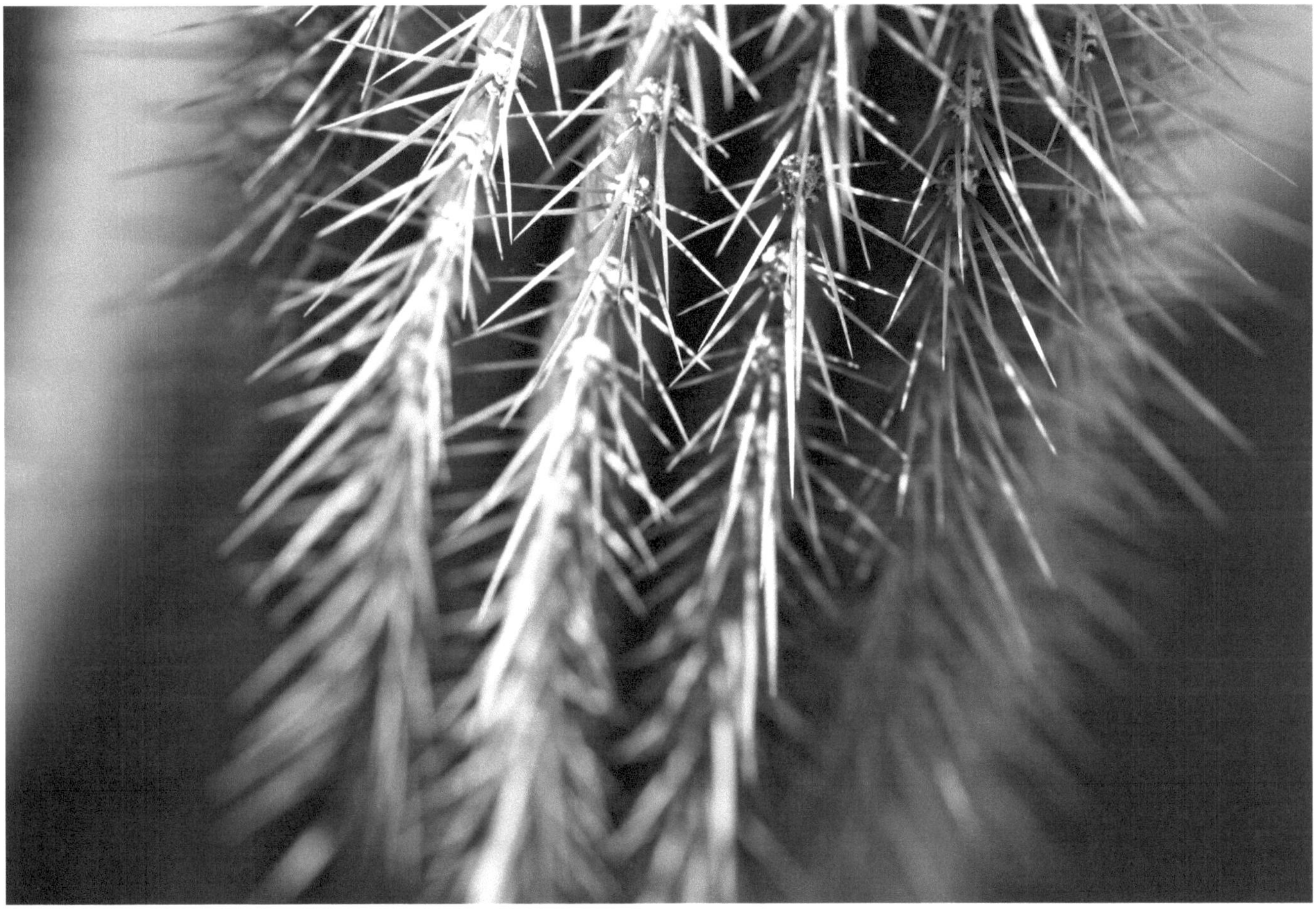
4070

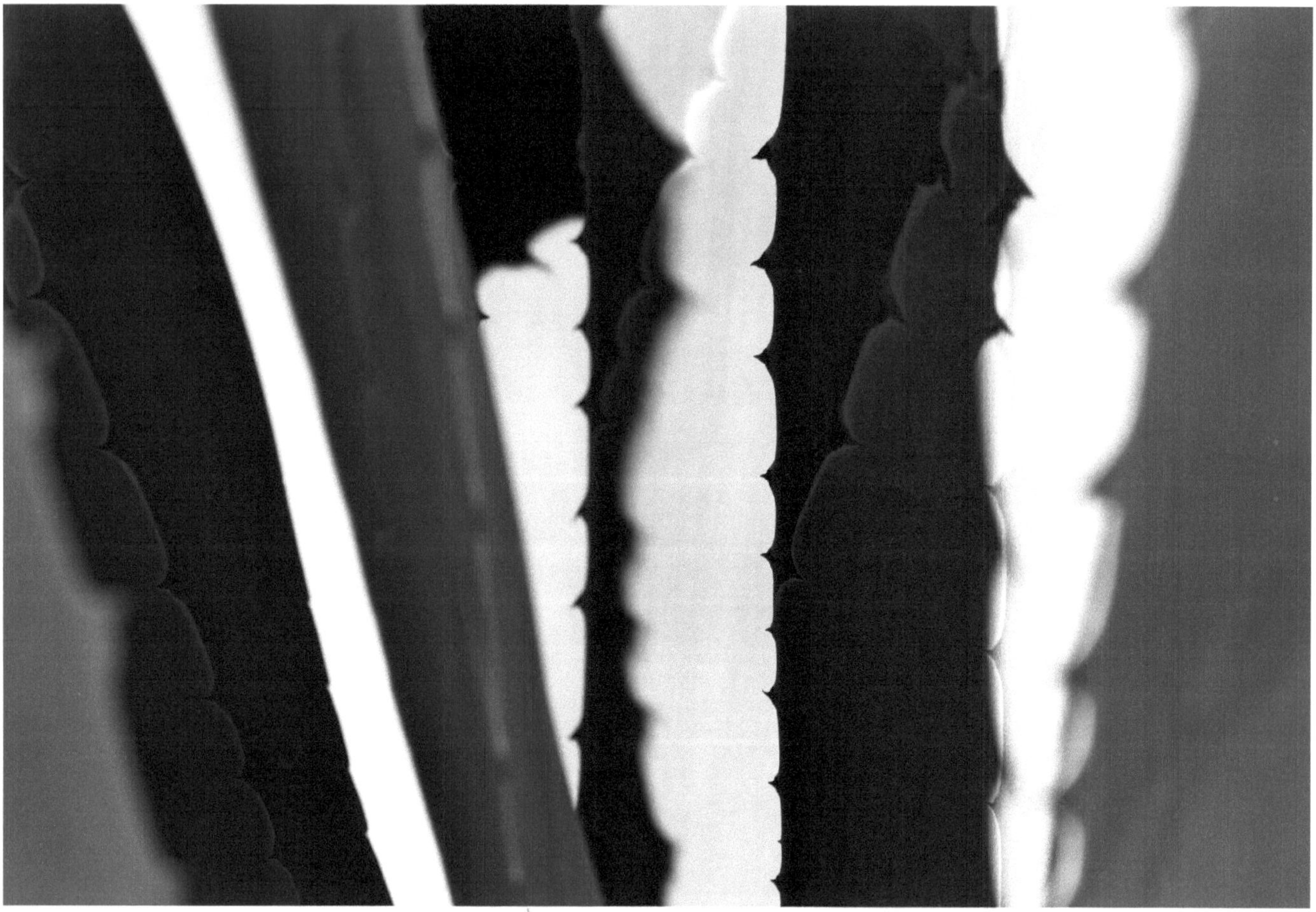

4099

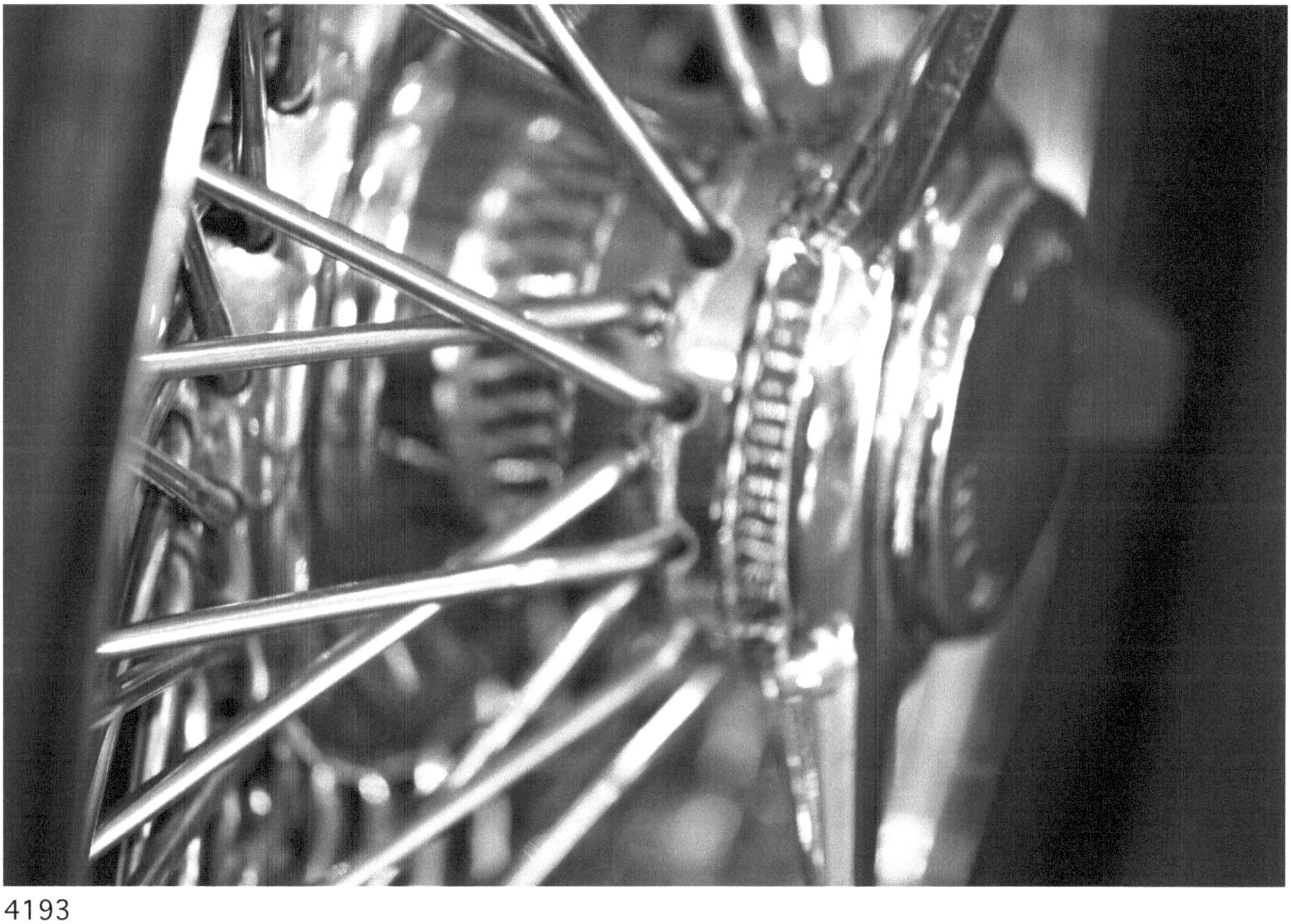

4193

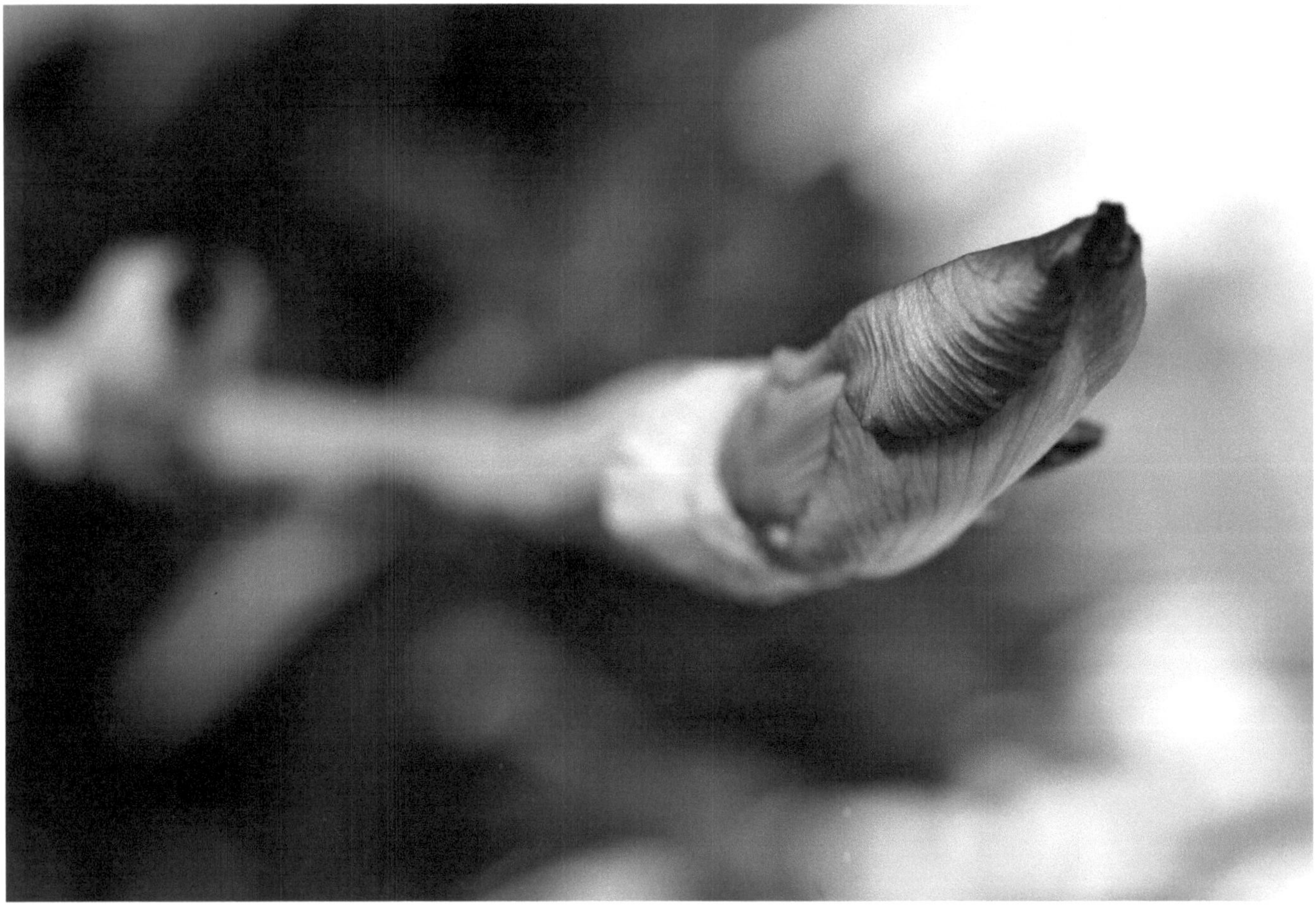

5492

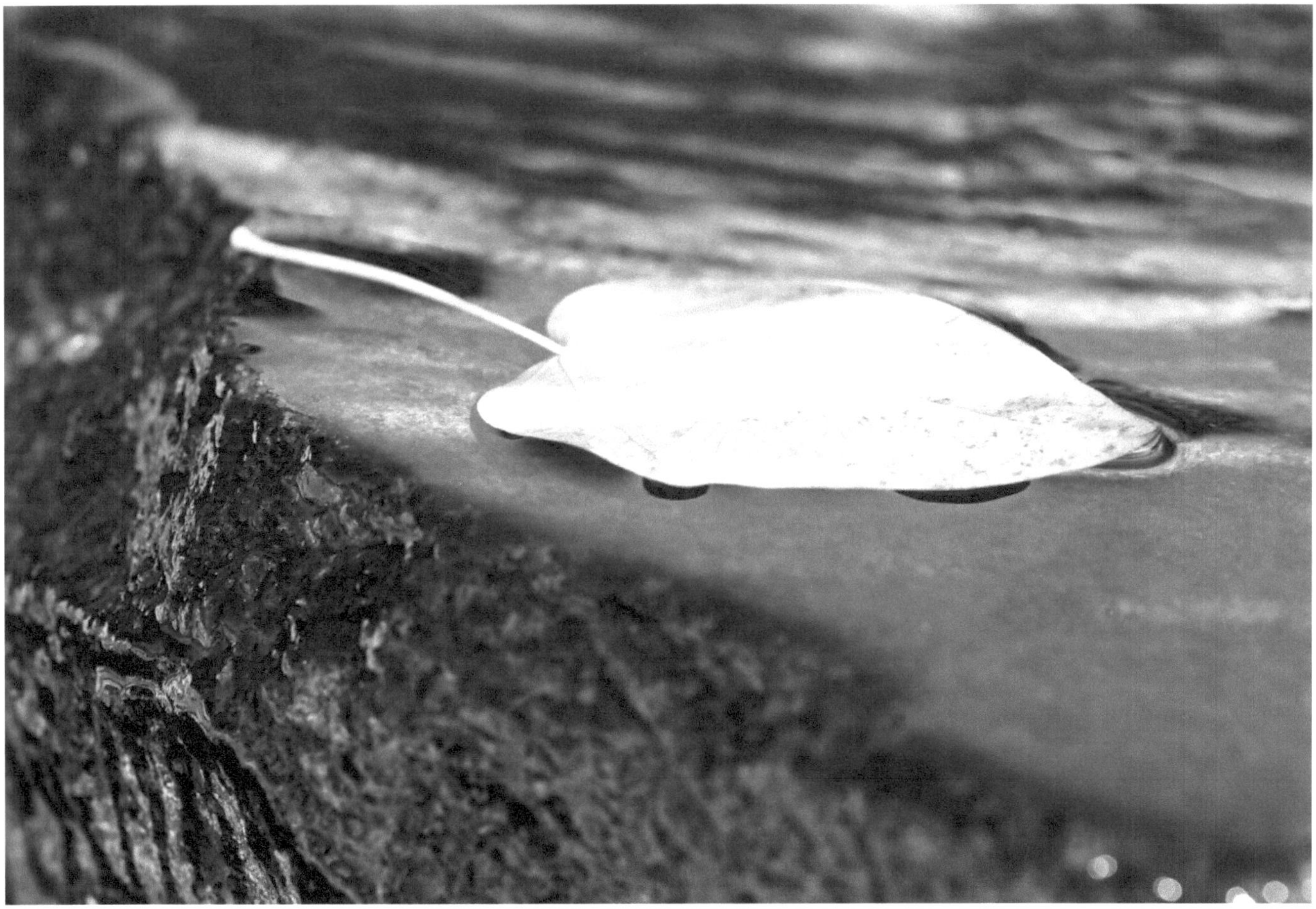

5750

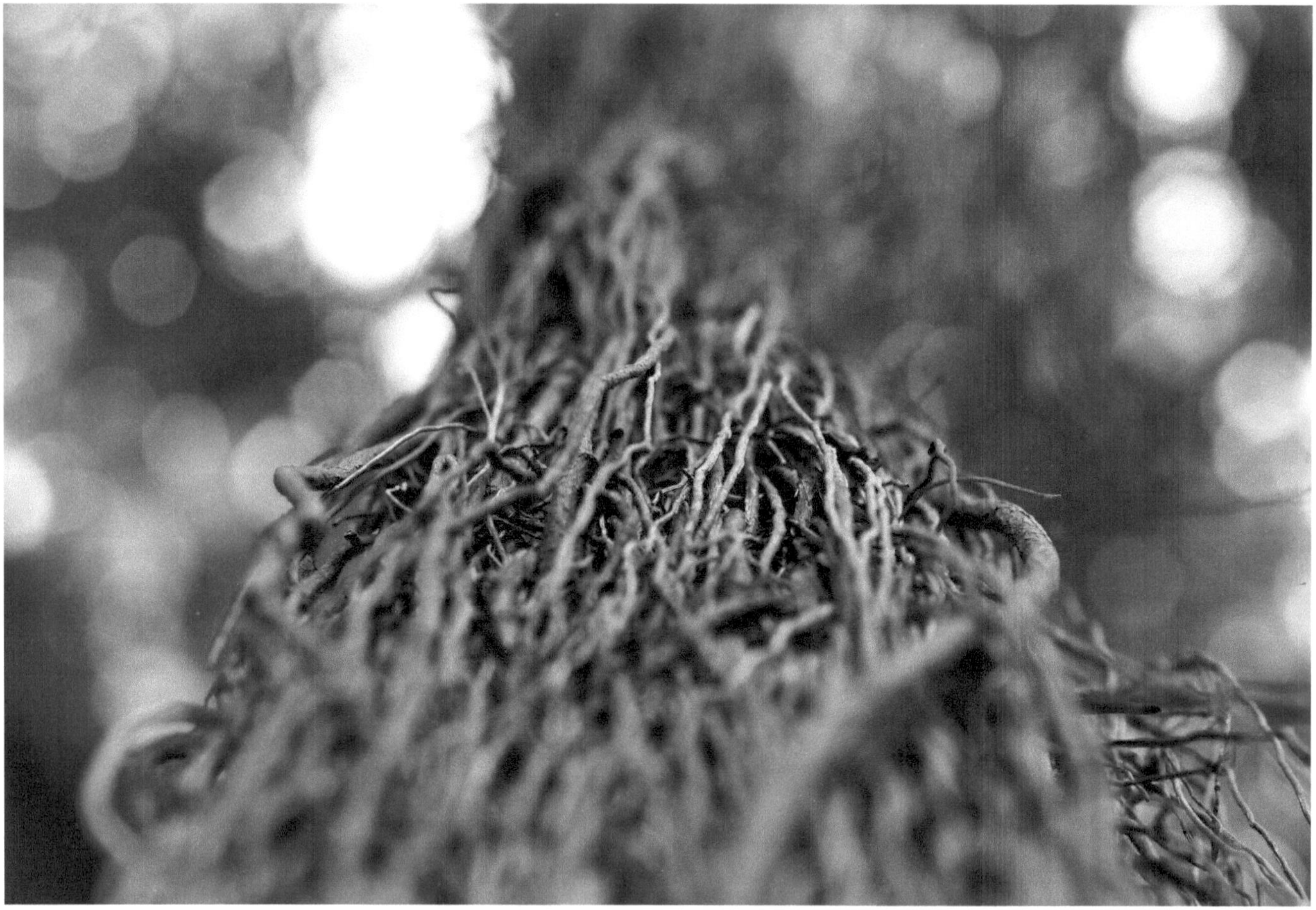

5811

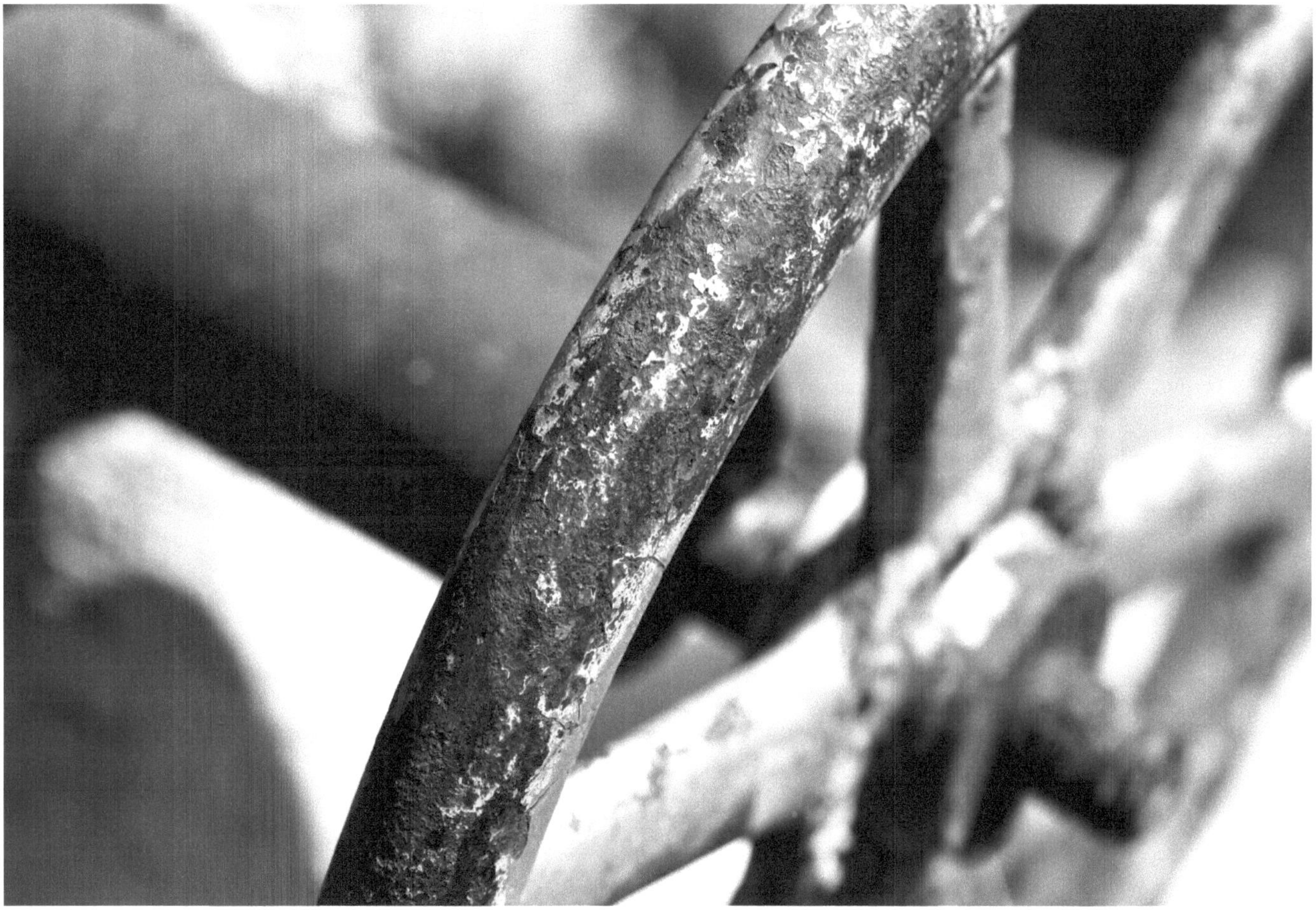

6095

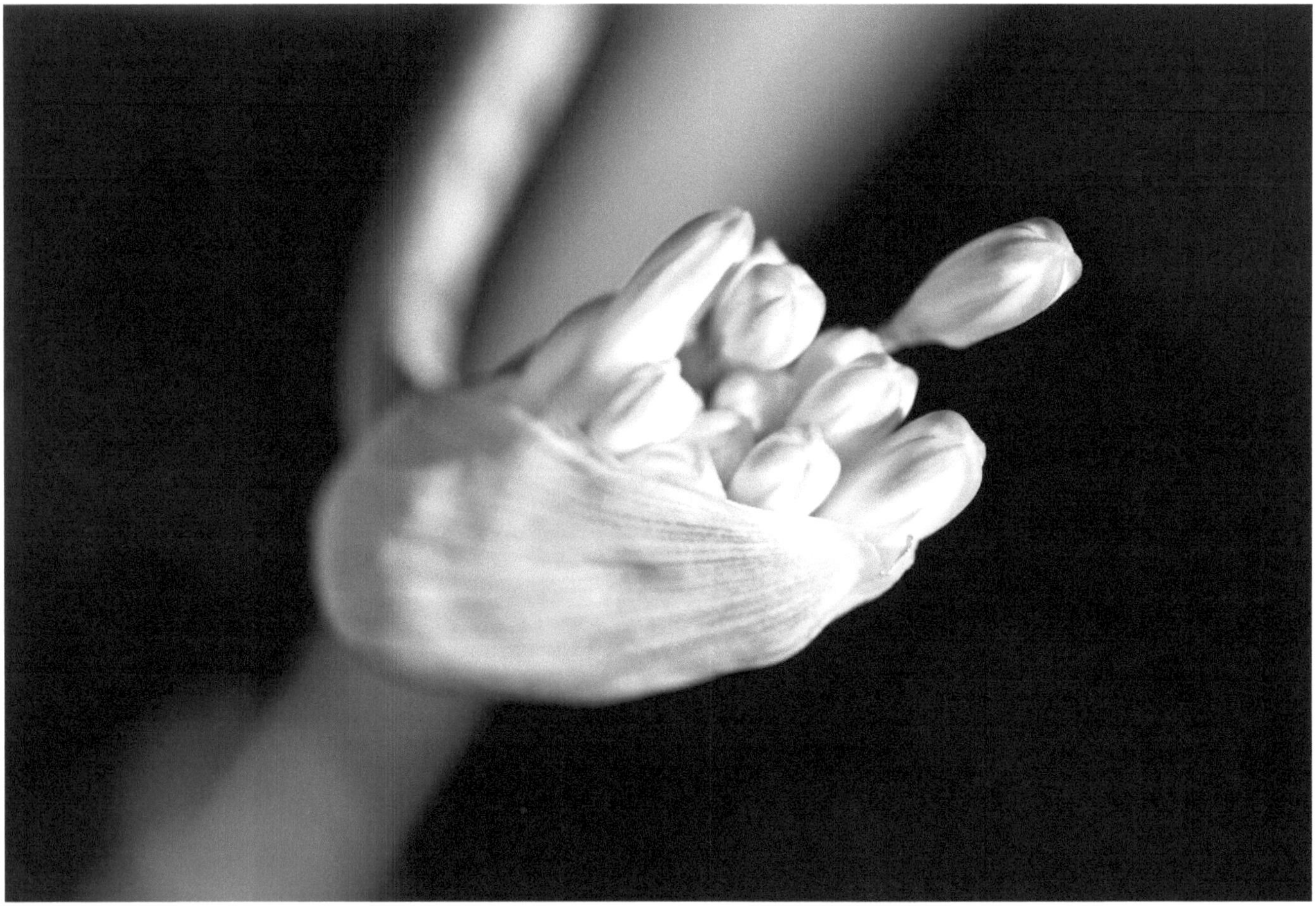

8407

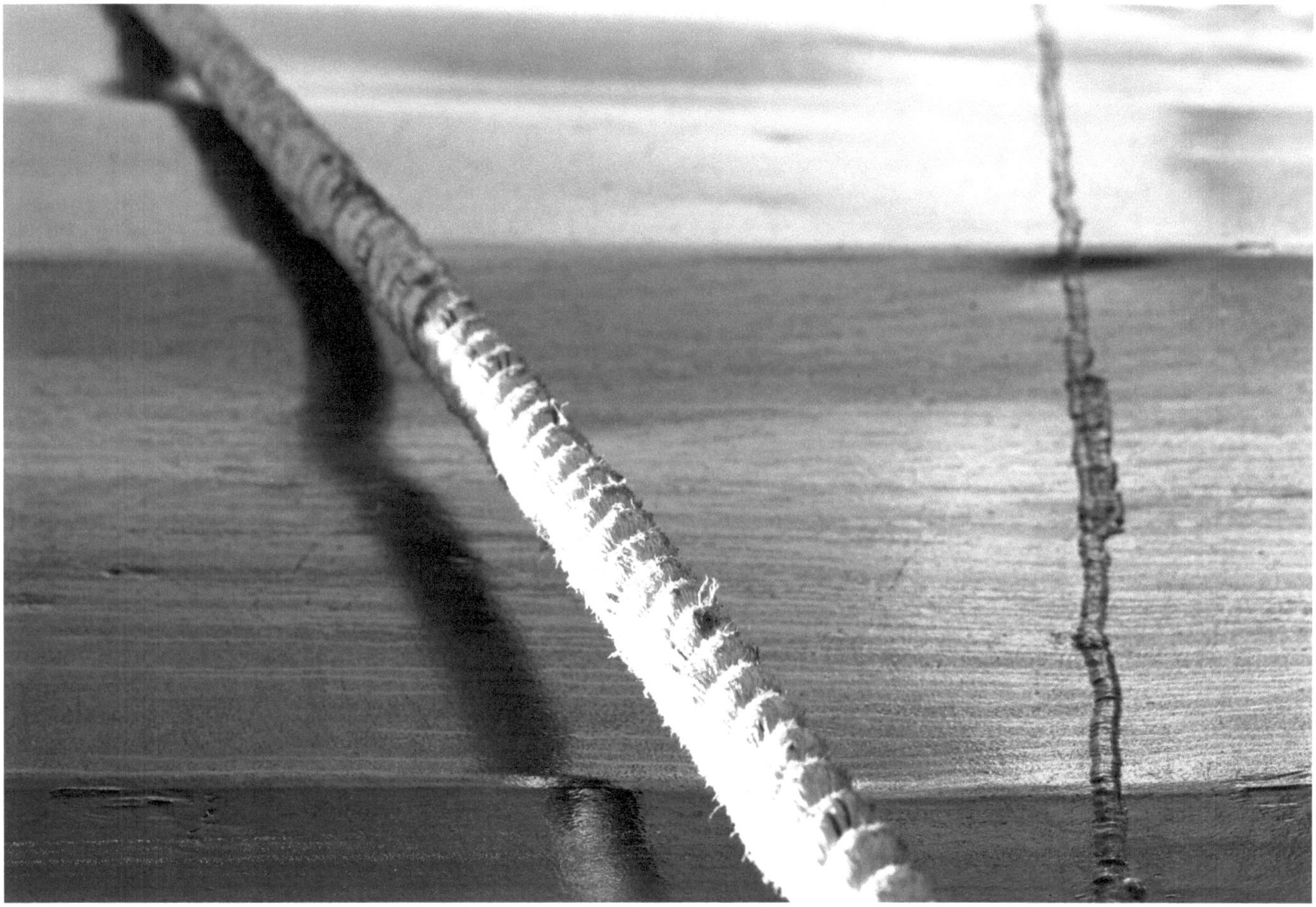

8470

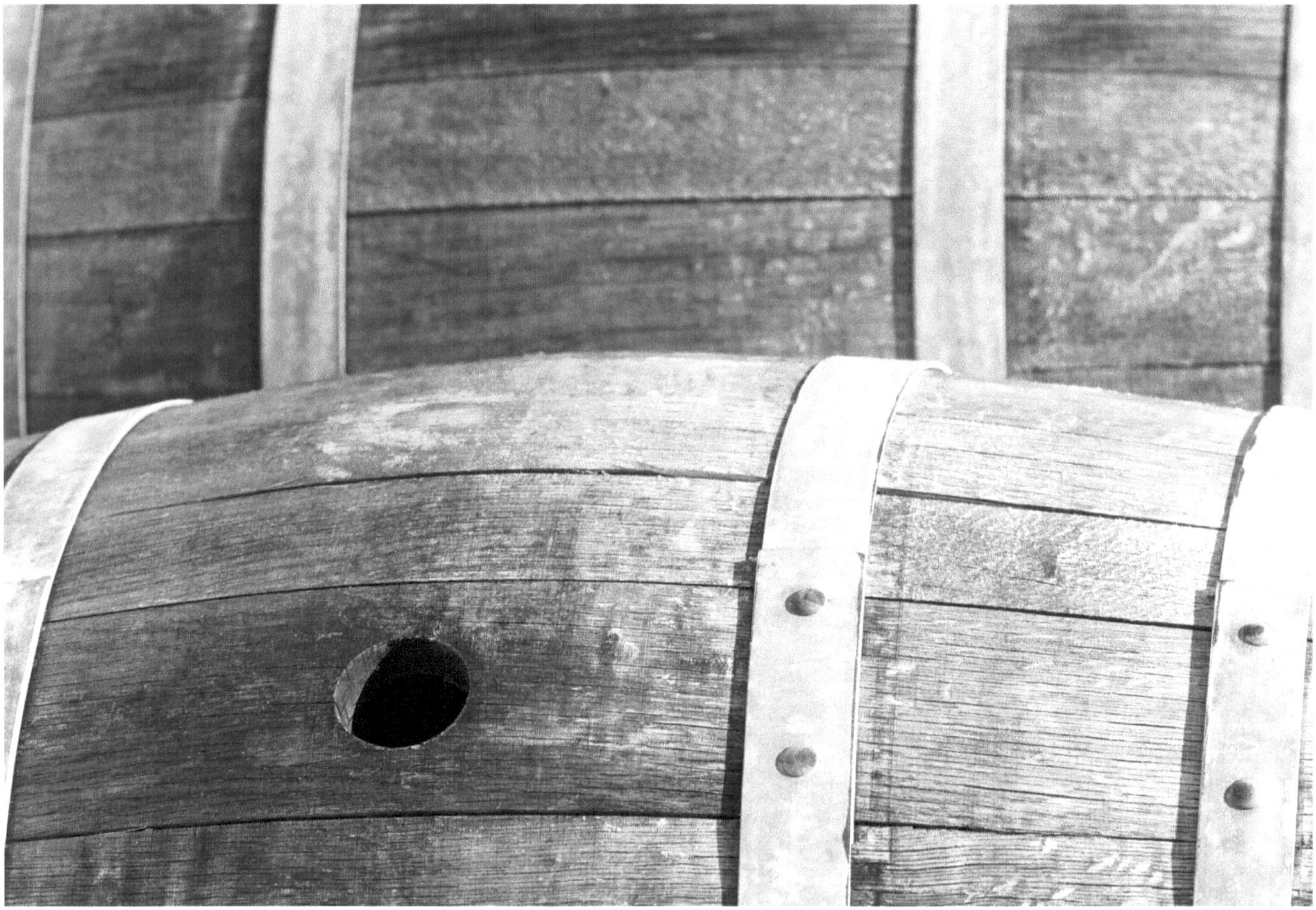

8815

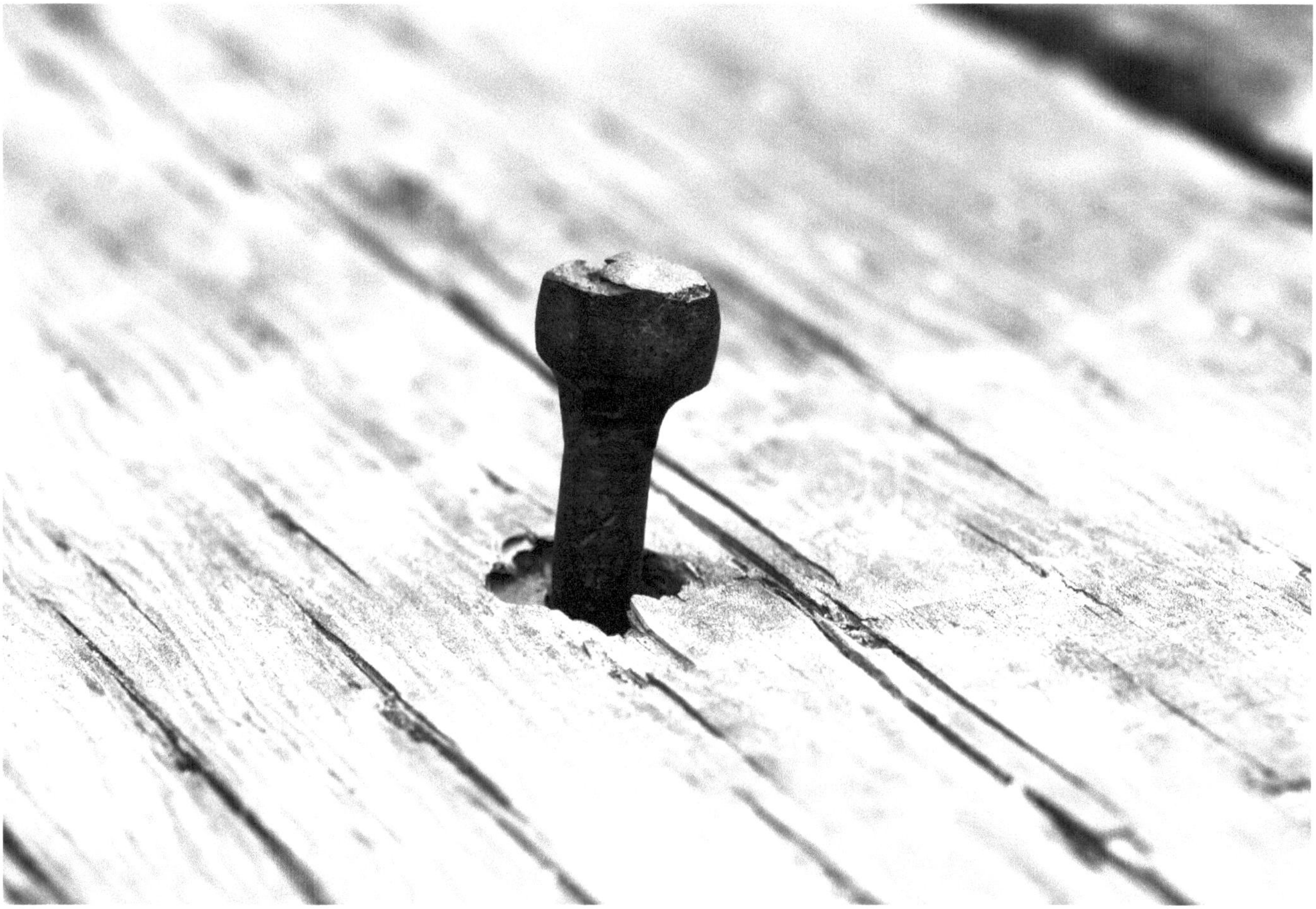

9024

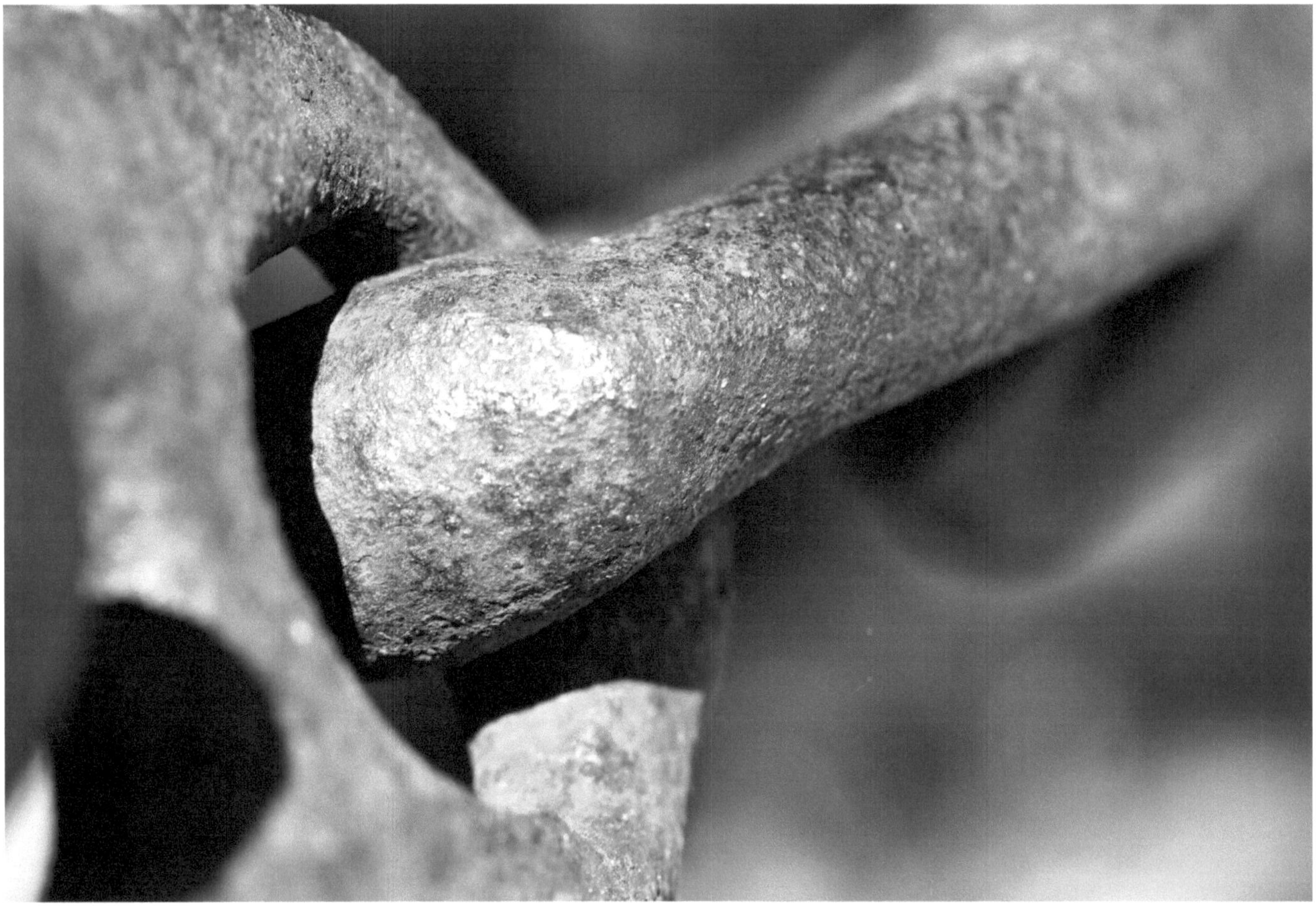

9353

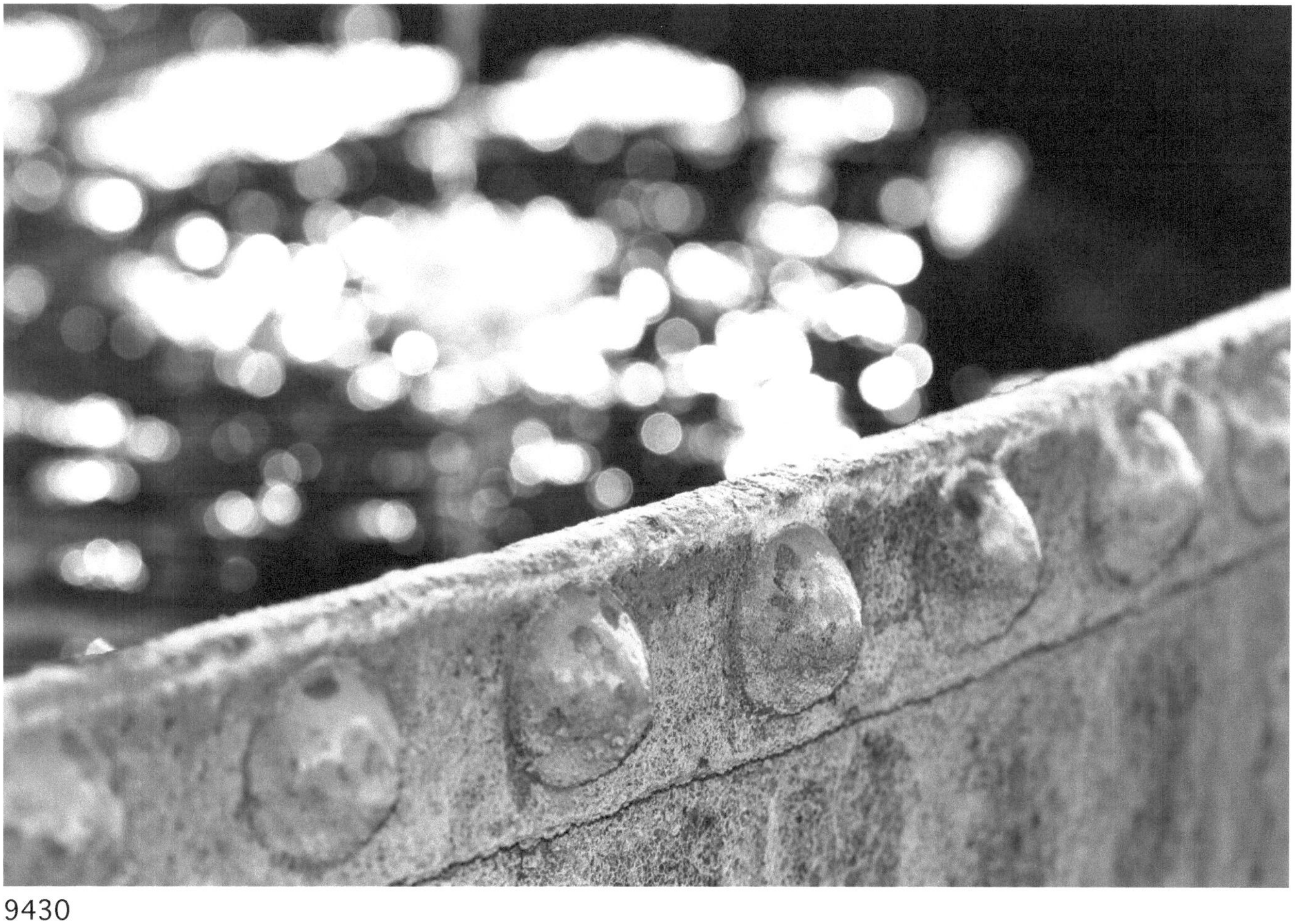

9430

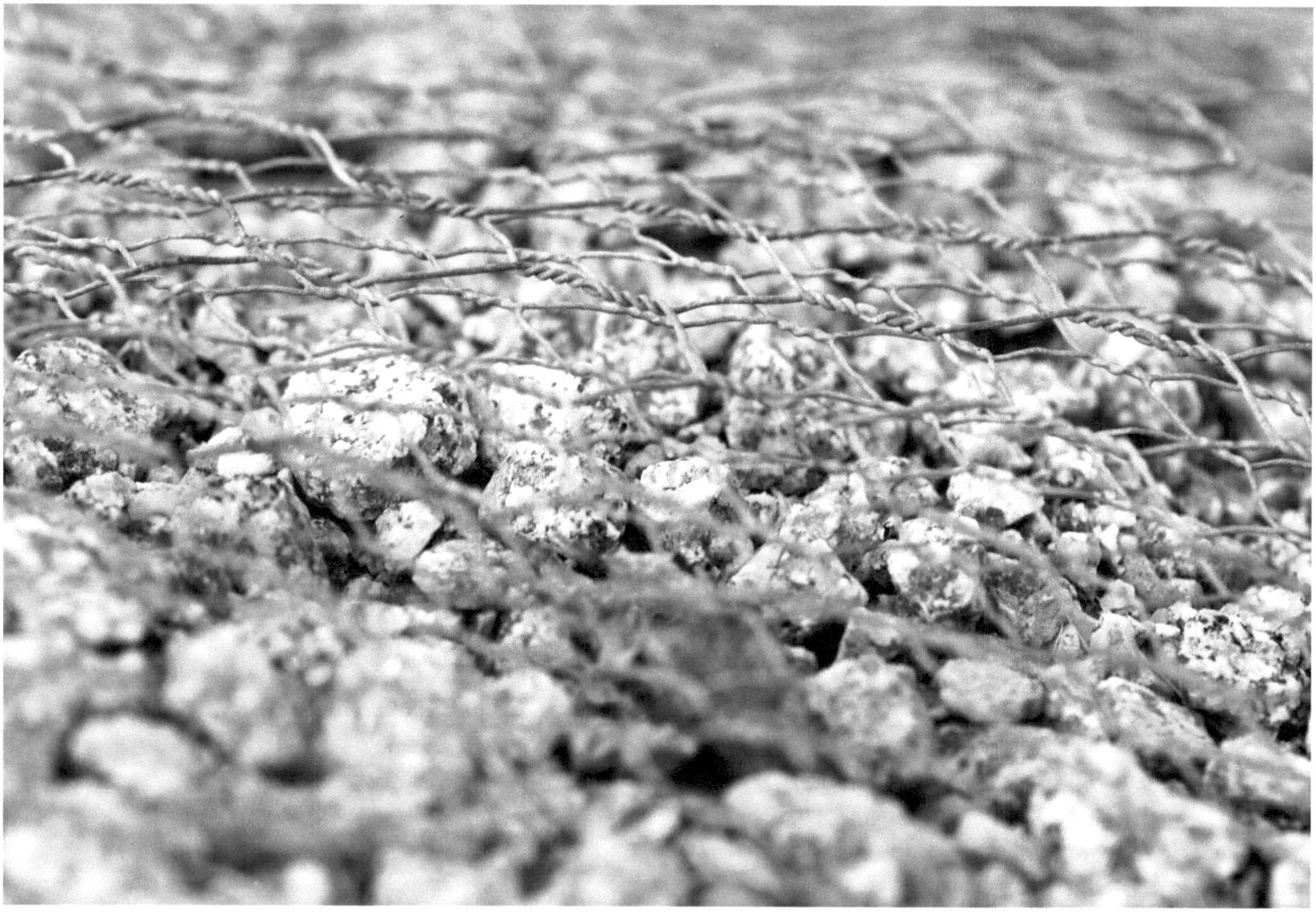

9970

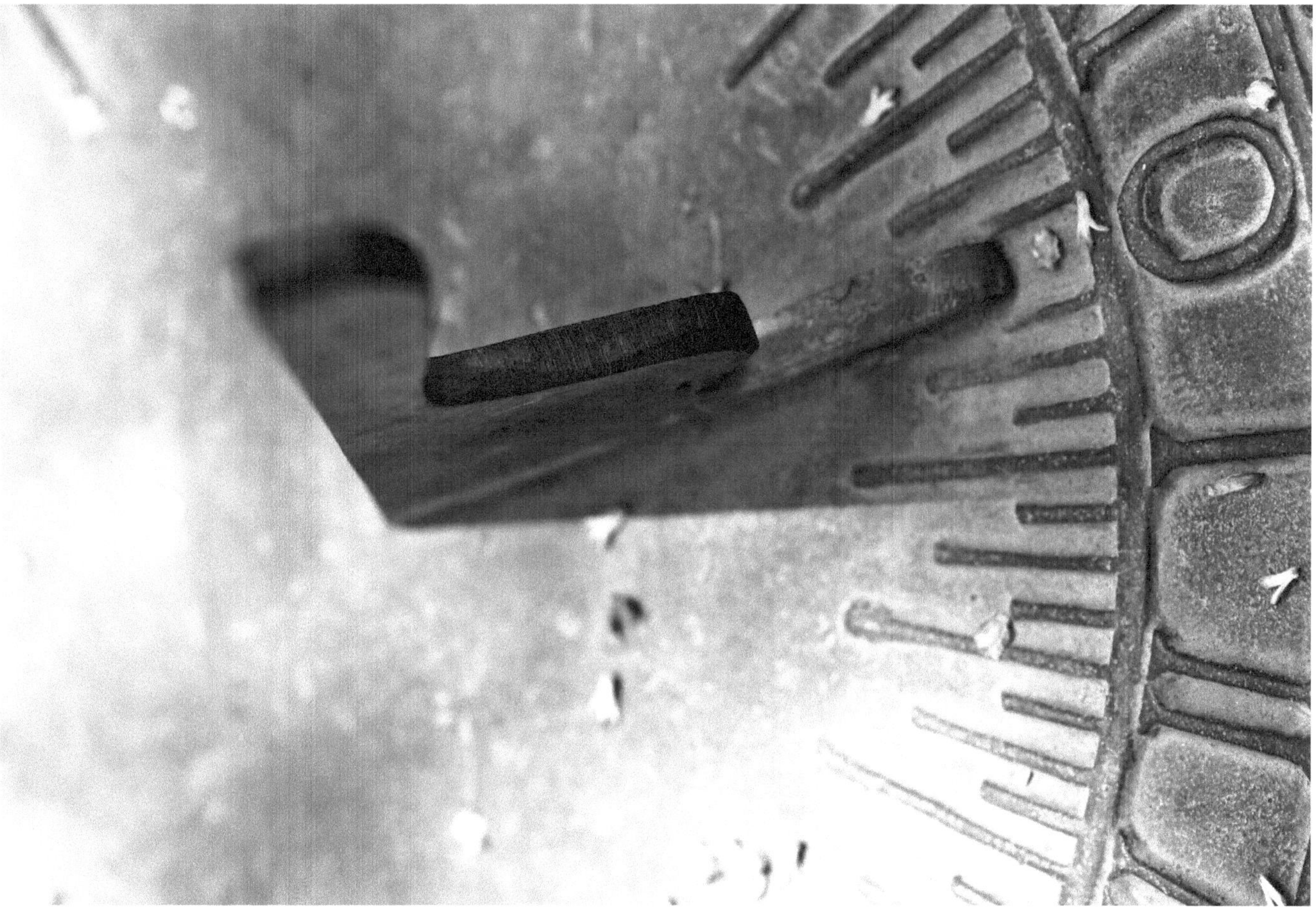

10002

www.ingramcontent.com/pod-product-compliance
Lightning Source LLC
Chambersburg PA
CBHW050415180526
45159CB00005B/2280